DATE DUE

DISCARDED

615
DeS   DeStefano, Susan
c.2   Focus on medicines

Focus on Medicines

Focus on Medicines

A Drug-Alert Book

Susan DeStefano
Illustrated by David Neuhaus

TWENTY-FIRST CENTURY BOOKS
FREDERICK, MARYLAND

Published by
Twenty-First Century Books
38 South Market Street
Frederick, Maryland 21701

Printed in the United States of America

10 9 8 7 6 5 4 3 2 1

Library of Congress Cataloging in Publication Data

DeStefano, Susan
Focus on Medicines
Illustrated by David Neuhaus

(A Drug-Alert Book)
Summary: Discusses different kinds
of medicines, their history, and their uses.
1. Drugs—Juvenile literature.
[1. Drugs. 2. Medicine.]
I. Neuhaus, David, ill. II. Title.
III. Series: The Drug-Alert Series.
RM301.17.B43   1991
615'.1—dc20   90-11273 CIP AC
ISBN 0-941477-94-0

Table of Contents

Introduction

"Baby Saved by Miracle Drug!" "Drug Bust at Local School!" Headlines like these are often side by side in your newspaper, or you may hear them on the evening news. This is confusing. If drugs save lives, why are people arrested for having and selling them?

The word "drug" is part of the confusion. It is a word with many meanings. The drug that saves a baby's life is also called a medicine. The illegal drugs found at the local school have many names—names like pot, speed, and crack. But one name for all of these illegal drugs is dope.

Some medicines you can buy at your local drugstore or grocery store, and there are other medicines only a doctor can get for you. But whether you buy them yourself or need a doctor to order them for you, medicines are made to get you healthy when you are sick.

Dope is not for sale in any store. You can't get it from a doctor. Dope is bought from someone called a "dealer" or a "pusher" because using, buying, or selling dope is against the law. That doesn't stop some people from using dope. They say they do it to change the way they feel. Often, that means they are trying to run away from their problems. But when the dope wears off, the problems are still there—and they are often worse than before.

There are three drugs we see so often that we sometimes forget they really are drugs. These are alcohol, nicotine, and caffeine. Alcohol is in beer, wine, and liquor. Nicotine is found in cigarettes, cigars, pipe tobacco, and other tobacco products. Caffeine is in coffee, tea, soft drinks, and chocolate. These three drugs are legal. They are sold in stores. But that doesn't mean they are always safe to use. Alcohol and nicotine are such strong drugs that only adults are allowed to buy and use them. And most parents try to keep their children from having too much caffeine.

Marijuana, cocaine, alcohol, nicotine, caffeine, medicines: these are all drugs. All drugs are alike because they change the way our bodies and minds work. But different drugs cause different changes. Some help, and some harm. And when they aren't used properly, even helpful drugs can harm us.

Figuring all this out is not easy. That's why The Drug-Alert Books were written: so you will know why certain drugs are used, how they affect people, why they are dangerous, and what laws there are to control them.

Knowing about drugs is important. It is important to you and to all the people who care about you.

David Friedman, Ph.D.
Consulting Editor

Dr. David Friedman is Associate Professor of Physiology and Pharmacology and Assistant Dean of Research Development at the Bowman Gray School of Medicine, Wake Forest University.

Medicine: The Drug That Heals

Long, long ago, before history was ever written, people discovered fire. The very earliest human beings learned that fire gave heat and light. They learned to use fire to keep warm, to cook their food, and to light up their homes. Fire was a helpful tool that improved their lives in many ways. People soon learned, however, that fire could also be harmful. When fire was not used carefully, it could hurt them. A fire, raging out of control, could destroy their homes, their forests, and even their lives.

Long ago, people also discovered medicine. And like fire, the discovery of medicine changed and improved their lives. Medicines helped people to get better when they were sick. Medicines helped to ease their pain when they were injured.

But just as people learned that fire can be dangerous, they learned that helpful medicines could also be harmful. That's because medicines are drugs. And like other drugs, medicines change the way the body and the brain work.

When they are used properly, medicines help to heal the sick and the injured. They can improve people's health and lives. But when they are not used carefully, medicines can do just the opposite. They can damage people's health and lives. They can make people sick.

This is the problem with medicines. Although they are meant to be useful and helpful, medicines can also be harmful and dangerous. And this is why you need to know the facts about medicines. You need to know the facts about medicines so that you can learn how to use them properly.

You need to know what the different types of medicines are and what they do. You need to know how some medicines help the body when it is sick and how others keep the body from getting sick in the first place. You need to know that some medicines cause unintended reactions, or side effects.

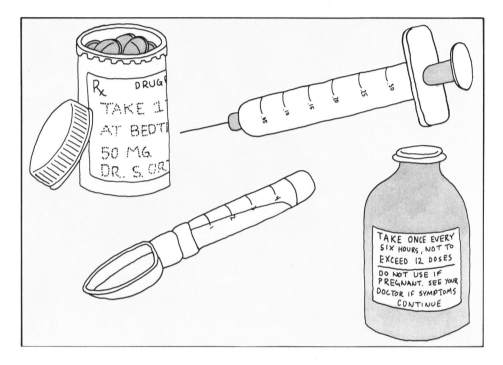

You also need to remember that medicines are drugs—drugs that can be both helpful and harmful. Like other drugs, medicines change the way the body works. Some medicines change the way the brain works, too. They can change the way people think, feel, and behave.

This book will help you learn about medicines. It will give you the facts that you need to understand what happens to the body when it is sick. And it will explain how medicines change the way the body and brain work and why they make people feel better.

This book will also give you the facts that you need to understand how medicines can hurt you if they are not used properly. And it will give you the rules for taking medicines safely. With this information, you will learn how to make safe and smart decisions about medicines. You will learn how to make medicines part of a happy and healthy life.

The Body and Sickness

People usually take medicine because they are sick. But how do people know when they are sick? How do they know that they need to take medicine? And how do they know what kind of medicine they need to take? To answer these questions, you first need to understand what happens to the body when it gets sick.

Most times, you know when you're sick. You know it because your body gives you signs. Your head might throb with pain. Your stomach might feel upset. Your skin might feel hot and tingly all over. You might cough and sneeze or have trouble breathing.

All of these signs are called symptoms. Symptoms are warning signals that some part of your body is not working in a normal and healthy way. You may not know what these symptoms mean, but your parents or the doctor will know. And they will also know whether or not the symptoms are serious enough that you need medicine.

Many times, symptoms are not the signs of a sickness that requires medicine. Sometimes, however, symptoms are the warning signs of an infection somewhere in the body. An infection is a sickness caused by very tiny creatures that have invaded the body. These invaders are so small that you need a microscope to see them. Scientists call these tiny creatures microorganisms, or microbes.

Many microbes are not harmful. Some actually help the body to work properly and stay healthy. But there are other microbes that cause infections and disease. Scientists call these harmful microbes pathogens. The rest of us usually call them germs. Germs are the kinds of microbes that make you sick.

There are two main kinds of germs: bacteria and viruses. Bacteria and viruses are germs that can cause infections, or contagious diseases. An infectious, or contagious, disease is the kind you can "catch" from someone else.

Bacteria are microscopic, one-celled organisms that live all around us. Bacteria grow quickly in warm, dark, moist places. The inside of your body is perfect for them! In just a few hours, a single bacterium attached to the lining of the lungs, ears, nose, or throat can reproduce itself and multiply into millions of germs. These germs make poisons, or toxins, that harm or kill healthy cells in the body. A person begins to feel sick as more and more of the body's healthy cells are damaged or killed.

There are several kinds of bacteria that cause disease.

- *Cocci* look like small round dots. They cause many diseases, including scarlet fever, strep throat, and kidney infections, among others.

- *Bacilli* look like rods, or short sticks. Some of the diseases they cause include lung infections, such as pneumonia and tuberculosis.

- *Spirilla* look like squiggles, or spirals. They cause blood infections and a form of jaundice, among other diseases.

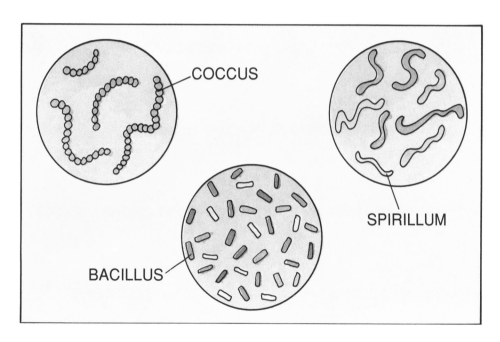

Viruses don't work the same way bacteria do. Viruses can grow only when inside a body cell. Once a virus germ slips inside the body, the virus invades a healthy cell. This healthy cell is called a host cell. Inside the host cell, the virus directs the cell to produce new viruses rather than new healthy cells.

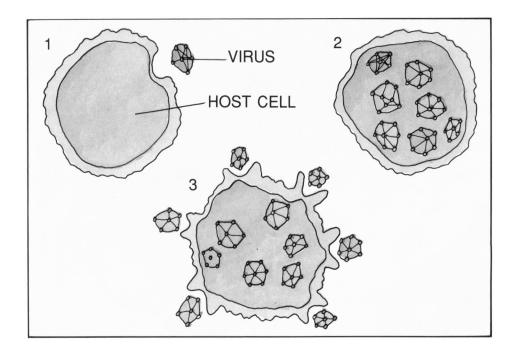

When the host cell releases these new viruses, hundreds of viruses fly toward other healthy cells. Each of these viruses invades a new host cell—and more and more viruses form. It doesn't take long for millions of viruses to spread throughout the body and make a person sick.

Viruses are the smallest living things. They are so small that it takes a special, "electron" microscope to see them. In fact, over 25 million virus germs can fit on the head of a pin.

But don't let their size fool you. As tiny as they are, they can knock you right off your feet! Viruses cause such diseases as the common cold, chicken pox, measles, and mumps and less common diseases, like viral pneumonia, hepatitis, polio, malaria, cholera, and yellow fever.

Although you can't see them, harmful bacteria and virus germs are everywhere. They fly through the air when a person sneezes or coughs. They swim around in the liquids that you drink. They lie on the surface of everything you touch. In fact, millions of harmful germs roam all over your skin, just waiting for a chance to get inside your body.

Your body usually does a good job of protecting itself against harmful germs. How does the body protect itself? It protects itself with a powerful, built-in defense system. This system is made up of an outer and an inner line of defense.

The Outer Line of Defense

You probably don't ever think about it, but your skin is working to protect you all the time. It covers your whole body and acts like a shield. Germs can't get through this shield, so they try to enter your body through openings such as your mouth, nose, eyes, and ears. But even these openings have built-in ways of fighting off germs.

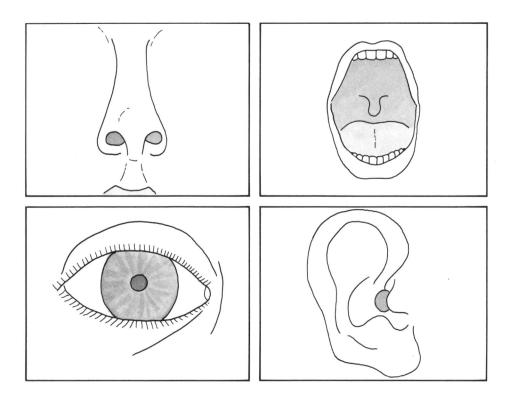

• The Nose

If germs get into your nose, they are usually trapped there by a sticky mucus that lines the inside of the nose and sinus passages. Tiny hairs, called cilia, that line the passages of the nose, sinuses, and the air tubes which lead to the lungs move the mucus-trapped germs from the nose to the mouth.

• The Mouth and Throat

The passages of your mouth and throat are also lined with mucus-producing membranes and tiny cilia. These cilia move mucus-trapped germs to the back of the throat, where they are swallowed. Strong acids in the stomach usually kill the germs before they can make you sick.

• The Eyes

When germs try this route, your eyelids and eyelashes protect you by blinking. If germs get by the eyelids, your eyes make tears, which can wash the germs away.

• The Ears

To keep out germs, your ears have a natural lining of tiny hairs and sticky yellow wax. The wax, which traps germs, usually works its way back out of the ear.

The Inner Line of Defense

Yet even with all of this protection, germs sometimes get through. They may enter through a cut or scratch in your skin. Or they may be so strong that stomach acids can't kill them. And some kinds of germs are just better at getting past the body's outer defenses than others. When this happens, the body's inner line of defense takes over.

The body has an incredible inner defense system to fight harmful germ invaders. This inner line of defense is called the immune system. Most of the time, you are not even aware that your immune system is at work. This defense system does its job so effectively that you never even know that germs tried to make you sick.

As soon as germs attack the body, the immune system is ready to fight back. The most important weapons in this fight are white blood cells. One type of white blood cell, called a phagocyte, travels through the bloodstream and is constantly on the lookout for harmful microbes. When these white blood cells meet any harmful germs, they quickly devour them. The phagocytes just gobble germs up. The word phagocyte comes from the ancient Greek word "phagos," which means "eater."

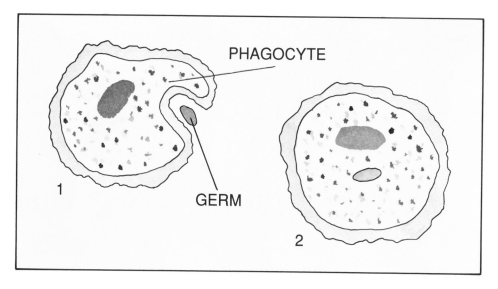

A person usually gets sick because there are too many harmful germs for the phagocytes to find and fight by themselves. Luckily, while the phagocytes are busily gobbling up these microscopic invaders, other white blood cells known as lymphocytes have joined the battle.

Lymphocytes have a special job in the immune system. Some lymphocytes, known as B-cells, help the body produce chemicals called antibodies. These antibodies travel through the bloodstream and attach themselves to the outer layer of germs. There are thousands of different germs, and each kind has a unique outer covering. Antibodies attach themselves to germs by recognizing these outer coverings, and a different antibody is needed to recognize and mark each kind of germ.

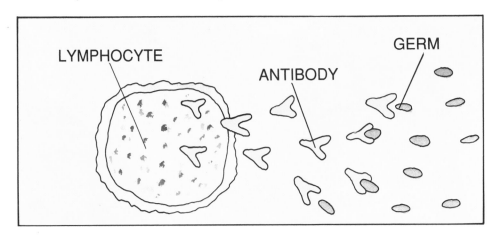

To fight thousands of different germs, the body's immune system produces thousands of different antibodies. When the right antibody finds the right germ, the antibody coats that germ with a chemical that marks the germ as harmful. This makes it easier for the phagocytes to find the harmful germs. It's almost as if the germs were carrying big signs that said, "Here we are, phagocytes. Come and gobble us up."

Your immune system would be a great defense against sickness if all it did was stop germs from making you sick. But it does more than that. The antibodies produced by the lymphocytes to fight a disease also give the body the ability to resist infection against that disease. This is called immunity. Some of the antibodies that the lymphocytes produce to fight a harmful invading germ stay in your body, ready to protect you from a future attack by that specific kind of germ. More important, if the body is attacked again by the same harmful bacteria or virus, the lymphocytes will produce the antibodies needed to give the body protection against that disease.

For example, if you get chicken pox, the body produces specific antibodies to kill the chicken pox germs. But once you get over a case of chicken pox, you probably won't ever get it again. You are now immune from chicken pox. If chicken pox germs try to invade your body again, the lymphocytes will recognize them immediately and quickly produce chicken pox antibodies so that the germs don't make you sick.

You may wonder, then, why you can get a cold over and over. If you have a cold once, why doesn't the body give you immunity against future colds? The answer is quite simple. It does! Once you get a cold, the immune system protects you from future attacks by the specific germ that caused your cold. But there are 200 different cold germs! When you get a new cold, it's because a new virus has found a home in your body.

It takes time for germs to make you sick. The period of time after you have been infected but before you feel really sick is called the incubation period. During this period, the germs are reproducing themselves and invading the various parts of your body. Soon, you will begin to feel the signs, or symptoms, of sickness. Some symptoms are due to the harmful effects of the germs; others are due to the body's fight against these germs. You've probably had these symptoms:

• Fever

Your body temperature is normally around 98.6 degrees (Fahrenheit). When harmful germs attack, however, the part of the brain that controls your body temperature causes the body to produce extra heat. This extra heat is what we call a fever. One thing a fever does is make the blood move more rapidly through your body. More white blood cells can then reach the parts of your body that are fighting harmful germs. The extra heat that comes with a fever also makes it harder for some germs to multiply.

• Chills

Sometimes your body makes the extra heat we call a fever by giving you the chills. The brain sends out signals to your muscles to shiver and shake. These rapid movements of the muscles, which give us the feeling we call the chills, produce extra heat. (That's also why you sometimes get the chills on a cold day.) When you have an infection, your body may stop sweating, too. Sweating is one way the body cools itself. When you stop sweating, your body is not cooling itself as quickly, and your body temperature rises. That's also why your skin often has a cold and clammy feeling when you are sick.

• Swollen Glands

The white blood cells that help to fight infection often gather and grow in the lymph system. The lymph system is a network of vessels that reaches almost every part of your body. Along this network are a number of glands, or nodes. The largest of these nodes are found in your neck, armpits, and groin. When you have an infection, there are so many white blood cells in these nodes that they become swollen.

• Pus

Pus is a yellowish, oozy substance that you sometimes see on a cut. It may look messy, but pus is a sign that your body's inner line of defense is working. Pus is the result of a hard-fought battle between phagocytes and harmful germs. The pus is a combination of dead germs, damaged cells, and phagocytes that have died while fighting to protect your body.

The body's natural system of defense works well most of the time. But sometimes the best that the immune system can do just isn't enough. The germs that attack the body are so strong and multiply so quickly that the immune system can't work fast enough or well enough. Then, the body needs help to fight off the germs. It needs the help of medicine.

Now, let's look more closely at some of the many kinds of medicine.

The Kinds of Medicine

In your home, as in almost every home, you are likely to find a medicine cabinet. Most of the medicines in this cabinet are "over-the-counter" medicines. People don't need to go to a doctor to get these kinds of medicines. They can buy aspirin, cough syrup, cold and allergy remedies, and many other over-the-counter medicines at the local drugstore or nearby super-market. Over-the-counter medicines don't prevent sickness or cure diseases. But they do help treat some of the symptoms people feel when they're sick.

Some of the medicines in this cabinet can only be obtained with a doctor's written order. They are known as prescription medicines. These medicines are stronger than over-the-counter remedies. When someone needs a prescription medicine, the doctor writes out an order, or prescription, for it. The doctor's prescription must be given to a pharmacist, who will prepare the medication. Only a licensed and trained pharmacist can prepare prescription medicines.

The pharmacist carefully reads the written prescription and prepares the medicine. On the label of the medicine container, the pharmacist types specific directions to the patient. The directions tell the patient when to take the medicine and how much to take. Because some medicines spoil quickly, the directions may tell the patient to store the medicine in the refrigerator. The pharmacist may also put a special sticker on the container that explains any side effects of the medicine.

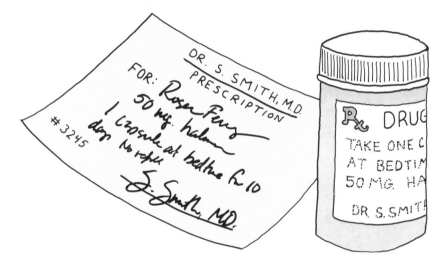

There are some kinds of medicines, including very strong painkillers and vaccines, that are never kept in the medicine cabinet. People can't buy them at a drugstore or supermarket. They are available only at a doctor's office or at a hospital.

Whether a medicine is in the medicine cabinet or not, it is important to know what it is and how it works.

How People Take Medicines

Before a medicine can help a person, it must enter the body. There are several different ways that medicine can enter a person's body.

- Some medicines, like cough and cold syrups and many prescription antibiotics, can be swallowed. Used this way, the medicine travels to the stomach and intestines, where it dissolves. It passes into the bloodstream and is carried to the rest of the body.

- Some medicines, like vaccines, can be injected with a hypodermic needle. They may be injected under the skin into muscle tissue, or they may be injected directly into the bloodstream.

- Some medicines can be put directly on the sick or injured spot, where they are absorbed by the skin. Ointments for cuts, burns, and rashes are applied directly to the skin.

- Some medicines can be sprayed directly into the mouth or nose. Medicines for colds, allergies, and asthma are sometimes taken this way.

GERM KILLERS

Most of the time, you get sick because harmful germs get inside your body and cause an infection. You may feel hot and feverish. You may feel tired and weak. You may feel achy and have an upset stomach. Let's face it: you feel sick.

If you have any of these symptoms, your parents may decide that it's time for you to see a doctor. The doctor will examine you and determine whether you have a bacterial or a viral infection.

If you are sick with a bacterial infection, your doctor may prescribe a medicine called an antibiotic. Antibiotics kill or weaken bacteria. Antibiotics help the body's immune system work faster and better to fight diseases. The most well known antibiotic is penicillin, but there are many others, such as erythromycin, streptomycin, and tetracycline.

Antibiotics are used to treat strep throat, bronchitis, ear infections, tonsillitis, pneumonia, and skin disorders, among many other kinds of infections. Antibiotics may be swallowed in tablet, capsule, or liquid form. Sometimes, when a person needs to get the effects of medicine very quickly, antibiotics are injected directly into muscle tissue or the bloodstream.

But some people suffer from unpleasant side effects when they take antibiotics. They may get stomach aches or become nauseous. Some people are allergic to certain antibiotics. They can break out in a rash or have trouble breathing. In some cases, allergic reactions to antibiotics can even be deadly. And certain antibiotics are unsafe for children or pregnant women.

Antibiotics are strong medicines that can help a person recover from an illness quickly. But as with all medicines, they must be taken carefully. And it is very important that people finish the entire amount of the antibiotic prescribed for them. Some people stop taking antibiotics when they start to feel better, but this only gives the germs a chance to grow back and make people even sicker than before.

What if the doctor discovers that you have a viral infection, such as chicken pox or the flu? What kind of medicine will the doctor prescribe for you then?

Unfortunately, there are very few medicines that work against viral infections the same way antibiotics work against bacterial infections. Instead, the doctor will probably tell you to get plenty of rest and drink lots of liquids. The doctor may prescribe a medicine that will lessen any serious symptoms, like headaches, fever, diarrhea, and vomiting.

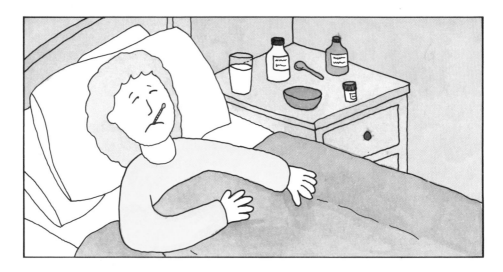

But more than likely, the doctor will suggest that you simply take an over-the-counter medicine to reduce the fever and aches that often accompany viral infections. Your own immune system will do the rest.

VACCINES

Although there are few medicines to treat viral infections, there are medicines that can keep you from getting some viral infections in the first place. And similar medicines can prevent some bacterial infections. These medicines are called vaccines.

Your body protects you against many diseases naturally. The antibodies produced by the lymphocytes to fight against a specific disease protect the body against future attacks by the bacteria or viruses that caused that disease.

But some diseases are so bad that it would be dangerous to get them even once. Vaccines are medicines that keep this from happening.

A vaccine is a medicine made from the dead or weakened germs of a disease. The germs in a vaccine medicine are so weak that even when they get inside your body, they don't give you the disease that they usually produce. The vaccine is simply too weak to cause the disease. But the dose of dead or weakened germs does make the lymphocytes produce the antibodies needed to protect the body from any future attacks of that specific disease.

Because the germs are dead or weakened, the immune system doesn't have to fight too hard to defeat the invading germs. If you are given a vaccine, you won't get sick, though sometimes you might get a fever and feel achy. Getting an injection of a vaccine to protect you against infectious diseases is called vaccination. When you were younger, you got your "shots." In other words, you were vaccinated against common childhood diseases such as mumps and measles, as well as polio, diphtheria, typhoid fever, and pertussis (also known as whooping cough).

You may have never even heard of some of these diseases. That's because vaccines have made them so rare. In the past, infectious diseases killed large numbers of people and threatened to wipe out whole countries. Today, even though there are vaccines to protect us, infectious diseases can still be dangerous to people who have not gotten their vaccinations.

COMMON VACCINATIONS		
Immunization:	Protection:	Side Effects:
DTP (or DPT)	diphtheria, tetanus, pertussis	fever; redness, pain, and swelling at the injection site*
OPV	poliomyelitis (or polio)	no significant common side effects
MMR	measles mumps rubella	fever; pain and swelling at the injection site

*In very rare cases, the pertussis vaccine may cause a severe reaction, requiring immediate medical attention.

PAINKILLERS

One of the most common symptoms people feel when they are sick or hurt is pain.

But what is pain really? And what can people do to get rid of it?

Pain hurts! And who needs that? Well, as a matter of fact, you do! Pain is necessary and helpful. Pain is like a warning sign that some part of your body is in trouble. It's a signal that you need help. If you didn't feel pain, you wouldn't know that you were hurt or sick. You wouldn't know when you should ask for help. And without help, the chances are that you might not get better.

You can't see pain, but you know it's there. You know it because you feel it. But not all pain is the same.

Imagine that your dad rides his bike up a long, steep hill. The next day, he may complain about the aching pain of sore muscles. Or what if your mother trips and breaks her ankle while she is out jogging? She would probably feel a deep, piercing pain. A carpenter who gets a splinter in his finger may feel a very sharp, stinging pain. A children's book editor working under the stress of tight deadlines may feel the pain of a throbbing headache. And your neighbor who is sick with cancer, a disease that attacks the body's healthy tissues, may suffer from terrible and constant pain.

It makes sense that different kinds of pain would require different kinds of pain treatments. Sometimes, rest is enough to treat minor pain, like the kind that comes from overworked muscles. At other times, a mild, over-the-counter painkiller may help a person feel better. And the deep pain that comes with a broken bone or with a serious illness such as cancer may require a stronger, prescription painkiller.

• Analgesics

Medicines that stop or ease pain are called analgesics. The most commonly used over-the-counter analgesic medicine is aspirin. Aspirin's scientific name is acetylsalicylic acid. It was first manufactured nearly a century ago in Germany and since then has been used all over the world.

Aspirin is dissolved by the stomach and sent through the bloodstream, where it quickly reaches the sick or injured spot that is causing the pain. It works right on that spot to stop the production of the chemicals that start pain messages on their way to the brain. Since the pain messages don't get sent to the brain, there is no feeling of pain. Aspirin can also reduce the inflammation, or swelling, that often causes pain.

Aspirin is a very helpful drug, but not everyone can take it. Some people are allergic to aspirin. For others, aspirin can upset the stomach, causing stomach aches and nausea. Also, young people should not be given aspirin when they have the flu or other viral infections. Taking aspirin for a viral infection can cause Reye's Syndrome, a very serious sickness that can damage the brain and even cause death.

Because of these unpleasant and dangerous side effects, scientists have developed medicines that act like aspirin but do not actually contain aspirin. Ibuprofen and acetaminophen are over-the-counter painkillers that do not contain aspirin. But they, too, can have harmful side effects and should always be used carefully.

For serious pain, over-the-counter remedies aren't always strong enough. In that case, a doctor may prescribe a narcotic painkiller. How do narcotics stop pain? Unlike aspirin and ibuprofen, which travel to the spot where the pain begins, narcotic medicines travel directly to the spinal cord and the brain, where they work to block pain messages from getting through to the different parts of the brain.

Morphine and codeine are natural narcotics made from the seed capsules of the opium poppy plant. These medicines are also known as opiates. Narcotics, or opiates, have been used to ease pain for thousands of years. Ancient people are known to have used the juice of the opium poppy to ease their aches and pains. Today, morphine, codeine, and some synthetic (or laboratory-made) narcotic painkillers are effective and valuable medicines. Doctors rely on these medicines to treat patients who suffer from serious pain.

Narcotics are safe when they are used under the watchful care of a doctor. But sometimes people misuse or abuse these drugs. They take too much, or they take them too often.

And when they do, they are also taking a big risk. Large doses of these medicines can cause serious injury to the body and brain. Too large a dose of an opiate can even cause death. And these drugs can be addictive. That means it can be very hard for people to stop using narcotic drugs once they start using them on a regular basis.

• Anesthetics

There are other medicines that doctors also use to prevent pain. These medicines are called anesthetics. They cause a loss of feeling, including the sensation of pain.

General anesthetics are powerful medicines that are used by doctors when major surgery is performed. These medicines depress, or slow down, the entire nervous system and cause a person to become unconscious, or "black out."

Local anesthetics work by blocking pain messages from leaving one part of the body and traveling to the spinal cord and the brain. They are often used during minor surgery and dental procedures. If you need to have a tooth filled, the dentist may give you an injection of Novocain to cause a loss of feeling in the area near the tooth.

COLD AND COUGH REMEDIES

Your nose is runny. You sniff and cough and sneeze. Your throat is sore and scratchy. And your head is so stuffed up it feels like the inside of a pillow.

You have a cold. An average, everyday, common cold. And you feel terrible!

Colds are caused by viruses, and there are lots of different cold germs around. Like other infectious diseases, cold germs are contagious: they are spread from one person to another. When a person with a cold sneezes or coughs, the germs fly through the air looking for another victim. You!

A cold can make you feel miserable. But because a cold is a viral infection, there are no medicines to cure it. It's up to your immune system to do the job. What about the shelves of cold and cough medicines in the drugstore? They can't cure a cold. They can only help to relieve some cold symptoms. Over-the-counter analgesics can reduce the aches, pain, and fever of a cold. Cough drops can soothe your throat; cough syrups can quiet your cough. And decongestants can relieve that stuffy, pillow-headed feeling.

These medicines can't make people better. They can only make them *feel* better. But that's important, too. When people feel better, they can rest easier, and this helps the immune system to do its job.

Most of these remedies are over-the-counter medicines. A doctor may prescribe a cough syrup with codeine for a painful cough that makes you very uncomfortable. But most doctors believe that getting lots of rest and drinking lots of liquids are the best "prescriptions" for the common cold.

ALLERGY REMEDIES

Your nose is runny again. You start to sniff and cough and sneeze. Your throat is sore and scratchy. And, once again, your head is so stuffed up it feels like the inside of a pillow.

But this time you don't have a cold. This time, you are having an allergic reaction. You have an allergy.

It's spring! The birds are singing. Flowers are blooming. The trees are once again turning green. It's such a beautiful world. That is, it's beautiful to everyone but you. You are allergic to pollen.

People with allergies suffer from an over-eager immune system. Normally, the immune system makes antibodies to protect us against harmful germs. But when a person has an allergic reaction, the immune system makes antibodies to fight against harmless things, like pollen, dust, animal hair, and some foods. The allergic reaction causes the body to produce a chemical called histamine. Histamine causes the unpleasant symptoms of an allergic reaction.

There is no medicine to cure an allergy. But as with cold remedies, certain medicines can help relieve common allergy symptoms. Because these symptoms are caused by histamine, the medicines that are most frequently used to relieve allergy symptoms are called antihistamines ("anti" means "against"). There are many over-the-counter antihistamine medicines. But like most other medicines, antihistamines can be harmful if not used carefully. If used too often, they can make a person's symptoms even worse.

A stuffy nose is bad enough. But some people have severe allergy symptoms. In this case, a doctor may write an order for a prescription allergy remedy. In the past, these medicines made people so sleepy that they couldn't even do their normal activities. Recently, however, scientists have developed allergy medicines that work well without producing drowsiness. And some people also get regular injections, or shots, to help them with their allergy symptoms.

Allergies can be very serious, and in some cases even life threatening. Some people are so allergic to insect stings that they can die from them. Other people have violent reactions to some medicines and even to some foods. People with these allergies must always be careful. Some may carry medicine with them at all times. Others may wear special bracelets that alert others to their medical problem.

As you can easily see, there are many different kinds of medicines. For as long as people have been getting sick, they have been looking for medicines to make them well again. The history of medicine is the story of mankind's search for an answer to the problem of disease.

It is a long and fascinating story.

The History of Medicine

From the time of the earliest cave dwellers to the 1800s, people did not know that germs caused disease. The treatment of disease and sickness was often based more on magic than medicine, more on folklore than facts.

For thousands of years, most people thought that disease was something they couldn't control. They believed that sickness was a punishment sent by angry gods or the unfriendly work of evil spirits. To cure sick people, they tried to please the gods or drive out the evil spirits from the body. This was often the job of the religious leaders of the ancient people. Sick people would pray to the gods of healing or seek magical cures from the tribal shaman, or medicine man.

But early medical treatments weren't completely based on magic and myth. Ancient people, for instance, discovered the first medicines. They found out that many plants could help them when they were sick.

A few of these natural medicines are still used in some form today.

- The Egyptians placed moldy bread on wounds to help them heal. The antibiotic germ killer penicillin is also made from mold.

- The Chinese brewed a tea made from the mahuang shrub. The stems of this shrub contain ephedrine, a medicine found in some modern cold remedies.

- The Sumerians used the juice of the opium poppy to ease pain. The narcotic painkillers morphine and codeine are made from the opium poppy.

- Native Americans chewed the bark of the willow tree to relieve pain. The bark of the willow tree contains salicin, a chemical used in making aspirin.

From the leaves of the foxglove plant comes digitalis, a medicine used for the treatment of heart failure. The bitter-tasting bark of the Peruvian cinchona tree gives us quinine, a drug that was used for many years to prevent or cure malaria. The ancient Egyptians used nearly 700 natural remedies made from plant sources. Medical books from ancient India list more than 500 plant remedies. And the writings of the ancient Greek doctors name more than 300 healing plants.

What these ancient people did not understand was *why* certain plants helped to make them feel better. They observed the result of using these natural medicines, but the cause of disease itself was a mystery to them.

Throughout the centuries, people continued to ask new questions about the cause of disease. They looked for answers inside the body. The ancient Chinese, Egyptians, and Greeks closely studied the organs of the human body. They looked for answers outside the body. The ancient Indians, Hebrews, and Romans observed the vital connection between personal and public cleanliness, or hygiene, and health. But without a scientific method, without scientific observation and proof, the discovery of effective medicines would be, at best, a matter of trial and error. At worst, it would be a matter of luck.

Without science, people remained powerless to prevent and cure most disease.

As the history of medicine shows, the discovery of a new medicine is a combination of hard work and good fortune. It is a combination of many people sharing scientific results and one creative pioneer struggling to see a medical vision come true. It is a combination of years of work and one startling moment of truth. Hundreds of people have contributed to the history of medicine.

Let's look at a few of them.

Hippocrates and Galen

One ancient physician who sought to learn the cause of disease was the Greek doctor Hippocrates. Born in the fifth century B.C., Hippocrates did not believe that angry gods or evil spirits caused disease. Instead, he believed that there were natural causes for disease and that there was a "healing power of nature." Hippocrates stressed the natural sources of health: a good diet, plenty of rest, and fresh air. He prescribed simple, natural medicines as needed, but he tried not to give strong drugs (like opiates) unless nothing else worked. Above all, Hippocrates believed that medical care was a science. Medical knowledge, he taught, could only be obtained through very close observation of the sick.

The most famous physician during the time of the ancient Romans was Galen. Galen was one of the first doctors to base his ideas about health and sickness on scientific research. He performed numerous experiments on animals and used his findings to describe the human body. Galen believed that sickness meant that the body was somehow "out of balance," and he thought that medicines should work to restore the body's natural balance. Though many of his ideas about the human body were wrong, Galen's influence was very far reaching. His understanding of disease was accepted for 1,400 years.

Anton van Leeuwenhoek

In the 1400s and 1500s, there was a remarkable burst of interest in the scientific observation of the human body. The most famous artists of the Renaissance drew the human form in great detail. The artists of the time (including such well-known painters and sculptors as Michelangelo, Raphael, and Leonardo da Vinci) made hundreds of sketches of every part of the body. And scientists dissected, or cut open, dead bodies to observe the inner workings of the body. In 1543, a major milestone in the history of medicine occurred when a scientist named Andreas Vesalius published the first complete textbook of human anatomy, or the study of the human body. Every remarkable drawing was based on his firsthand observations.

But it was not until the 1600s that scientific observation made its greatest breakthrough. It was around 1675 that Anton van Leeuwenhoek, a Dutch cloth merchant, built a microscope powerful enough to magnify objects up to 270 times. It was powerful enough, in other words, to see a world that was previously unseen; it was powerful enough to explore a world that was previously unknown.

Leeuwenhoek was the first to see this world, and every object he looked at showed him how remarkable this invisible world really was. He studied the stinger of a bee, the head of a fly, the hairs of a sheep, the muscles of a whale, the legs of a louse, and the eyes of an ox. He even studied his own skin.

But the most amazing discovery of all involved a simple glass of rain water. Never again would anything be so simple. For what Leeuwenhoek saw in that glass of water was a world of living creatures. He was the first person to see the invisible world of microorganisms. Fascinated by these creatures, he drew hundreds of pictures of them and wrote careful descriptions. He named them his "animacula," or "little animals."

It was a discovery that would forever change the history of medicine. Yet almost 200 years would pass before scientists understood that some microorganisms were actually disease-causing germs. And, in the meantime, infectious and deadly diseases like cholera, typhus, and tuberculosis would continue to kill thousands of people each year.

But the scientific search for an answer—for a way to stop and prevent disease—would continue, too.

In that search, an English doctor by the name of Edward Jenner made a crucial discovery. In 1796, Jenner found a way to prevent the highly contagious disease smallpox. From the earliest times, smallpox had been a deadly and much feared disease. In the 1700s, smallpox was so common in Europe that about 60 million people caught it. And about one out of every five of them died from the disease.

Doctors didn't know what caused smallpox. But they did know that once people got smallpox, they didn't get it again. Edward Jenner noticed something else. He observed that the local dairymaids and farmers who got cowpox, a milder form of the smallpox disease, never seemed to get smallpox itself. Jenner wondered if having cowpox somehow prevented a person from getting the more serious smallpox disease.

There was only one way—a dangerous way—to know for certain. Jenner took cowpox germs from an infected dairymaid and vaccinated an eight-year-old boy (his name was James Phipps) with a dose of fluid containing the germs. James got a mild case of cowpox. Two months later, Jenner gave the young boy a dose of smallpox germs.

Then, Jenner waited and watched. The 12-day incubation period for the smallpox disease passed, and the young James Phipps showed no signs of being sick. The cowpox germs had made the boy's own immune system produce antibodies to the smallpox germs. James Phipps was safe from smallpox, and Edward Jenner had developed the world's first vaccine.

Jenner's discovery meant that for the first time doctors could prevent disease. But Jenner still had no idea how or why his vaccine worked. The discovery that would link germs to disease would not be made for 50 more years. It was not until 1877 that a Frenchman by the name of Louis Pasteur made that discovery.

Louis Pasteur

Louis Pasteur was born in Dole, France, in 1822. As a chemist, he worked with France's wine producers to find out why wine sometimes spoiled. He observed that there were microscopic germs in the spoiled wine. Through very careful experimentation, he proved that these germs caused the wine to spoil. He also discovered that by heating the wine to a high temperature and then sealing it, the germs were destroyed. This process became known as pasteurization. It's how the milk you drink today is kept from spoiling.

Louis Pasteur realized that if germs caused wine to spoil, they might be responsible for the spread of infectious diseases. He was also convinced that specific germs caused specific contagious diseases. Pasteur experimented with anthrax, a disease of sheep and cattle, and cholera, a disease found in chickens. He discovered that when he put the anthrax or cholera germs into healthy laboratory or farm animals, the animals got the diseases. In 1880, these experiments led to an even greater medical discovery.

Pasteur had been on vacation, away from his laboratory. Returning to his work, Pasteur mistakenly gave some chickens a mixture, or culture, of cholera germs that he had prepared before he left for vacation. But because these microbe cultures were old, they had gone "stale," and they had lost their power to cause cholera.

When he realized the mistake, Pasteur at once prepared new cultures and gave fresh germ doses to the chickens. But, then, something strange and startling occurred. The chickens did not get cholera. The weakened cholera germs had made the chickens immune to the new cholera germs just as Jenner's cowpox vaccine had made James Phipps immune to smallpox.

(To name this process, Pasteur used the term vaccination. He used that term to honor Edward Jenner's work with cowpox germs. The term "vaccination" comes from the Latin word "vacca," which means "cow.")

But Pasteur understood something that Jenner had not. He knew that the weakened germs of the disease provided protection against cholera. Now, he had to prove it to the world. So Pasteur undertook a bold and dramatic experiment with deadly anthrax germs. On May 31, 1881, in front of a large and curious crowd, he gave a dose of anthrax germs to two sets of sheep: one set had been vaccinated earlier with a dose of weakened germs and one set had not been vaccinated.

On June 1, Pasteur's assistants found that some of the sheep which had been vaccinated looked sick and feverish. Pasteur was very troubled. Was he wrong after all? But early the next morning, June 2, 1881, Pasteur received a telegram from his assistants:

"Of the 25 unprotected sheep, 18 are already dead, and the others are dying. But all the vaccinated sheep are on their feet. A brilliant success!"

It was a great triumph for Pasteur and a moment of great importance in the history of medicine. Now, at last, a process had been developed that offered protection against disease. There was hope, at last, that the same protection would soon be offered against other diseases. Again, it was Louis Pasteur who led the search for new medicines.

In 1885, Pasteur prepared a vaccine against the dreaded disease of rabies. Rabies is a deadly virus, spread by infected animals, that travels through a person's nervous system to the brain. In the 1800s, a person with rabies was almost certain to die. When Joseph Meister, a young German boy, was bitten by a rabid dog, his mother brought him to see the great French scientist. She had heard that Pasteur was working on a new treatment for rabies. She knew it was untested on humans. But she also knew it was her son's only hope.

On July 6, 1885, Pasteur looked at the small boy and his dreadful wounds. After consulting medical doctors, Pasteur made up his mind. He would be taking a big risk in testing the vaccine this way. But without help, the young boy would almost surely die. He decided to give the rabies vaccine to Joseph Meister.

And then, like Jenner before him, he waited and watched. By the end of several weeks, Joseph had completely recovered. To people everywhere, it seemed like a miracle. But to Louis Pasteur, it was no miracle. It was the result of years of work. It was the result of years of studying the effect that microbes had on laboratory and farm animals. It was the result of a lifelong commitment to science.

Pasteur's brilliant success encouraged other scientists to continue the search for disease-causing germs. And it gave them a new understanding of disease, one that would help them find medicines to fight diseases that had plagued the world for thousands of years.

Alexander Fleming

It may be hard for you to realize what the world would be like without antibiotics. Before the discovery of penicillin, the immune system had to fight disease-causing germs on its own. The defenses of the body were often strong enough to fight invading microbes, but if the harmful germs were too strong, there was little the body could do to protect or heal itself. Without safe and effective medicines to prevent the spread of germs, whole populations were defenseless against outbreaks of cholera, bubonic plague, dysentery, diphtheria, and many other diseases. A British doctor by the name of Alexander Fleming helped to change that.

In the fall of 1928, Fleming was busy in his laboratory. He was growing the disease-causing bacteria staphylococci. Fleming was conducting a series of experiments to see if he could somehow weaken the "staph" germs and thus remove a major threat to human health. But it was often a frustrating business. Fleming had to repeat many experiments because strange microbes would float down onto the dishes used to grow germs—and ruin his microbe cultures.

One day, he was about to throw out one of these ruined experiments because it had mold growing all over it. Mold is a very tiny and simple plant that has no chlorophyll (green coloring), so it cannot make its own food. Mold floats through the air, and when it lands on something it can use as food, it grows and multiplies. Molds live all around us. You may have seen mold on stale bread or leftovers in the refrigerator.

But Fleming didn't throw out the ruined culture. Because he was a careful scientist, Fleming took one more look at the culture under his microscope. There was something curious here, something strange and unexpected. Although most of the culture was cloudy with "staph" germs, the area around the mold was clear. A circle of clear liquid surrounded the mold—as if the "staph" germs had disappeared! And not far from this clear area, more germs were dissolving. It appeared that something from the strange mold was killing the deadly staphylococci germs.

Like Jenner and Pasteur before him, Fleming had made a remarkable discovery. But it was only the beginning. It was the beginning of more than a decade of hard work, of frequent disappointments, and of final triumph.

Fleming knew that the strange speck of mold that had found its way to his microbe culture belonged to a family of molds called penicillia. But he knew little else about it. He continued to grow the new mold and experimented with the "mold juice," or penicillin, that formed just beneath the mold.

- He tested penicillin on different bacteria and found that it destroyed or weakened a large number of different types of bacteria.

- He tested penicillin on samples of human blood and found that it did not harm healthy blood cells.

- He tested penicillin on healthy laboratory animals and found that it did not harm them.

Here, at last, seemed to be a drug that would destroy harmful germs without also destroying white blood cells, the basis of the body's own immune system.

But it was difficult for Fleming to convince other scientists that penicillin was a valuable medicine. There was simply no way to produce penicillin in large enough quantities to make it practical as a medicine.

It took more than a decade of research, the efforts of both British and American doctors, and the urgent need for new and more effective medicines brought on by World War II to find a way to develop large amounts of penicillin. In June of 1943, four different companies began to produce penicillin in the United States. And in 1944, Fleming saw the first penicillin factory in his own country begin to produce this badly needed medicine for England's soldiers. In that same year, almost 16 years after a strange speck of mold drifted down onto one of his microbe cultures, Fleming was knighted for his unique contribution to health and medicine.

The work of scientists like Edward Jenner, Louis Pasteur, and Alexander Fleming proved that medicines could be found to cure and prevent diseases. Their work provided a model for the many men and women who would seek medicines for diseases like polio, typhoid fever, and many others. And their work continues to provide a model today for the men and women who work to find new medicines, medicines that will one day put an end to diseases like cancer and AIDS.

To Your Health

You have learned that medicine is a drug that heals. You know that medicines work with the body's natural defense system to fight off the thousands of microorganisms that cause diseases. You know that some medicines keep us from getting sick and that other medicines are able to relieve the symptoms of sickness.

Most of the time, the immune system is able to fight off harmful microbes on its own. But at other times the body's own defenses are just not enough, and we get sick. When the body can't heal itself, we use medicines to do the job. Used properly and carefully, medicines help us get well again.

But you also know that medicines are drugs. Medicines change the way the body and brain work, and like all drugs, they can be dangerous to use. Medicines have side effects that can be quite serious. When they are not used properly and carefully, medicines can make people sick.

That's why it's so important for you to know and follow some basic rules about using medicines:

- Never take medicines without first checking with an adult. Not even an aspirin. Always ask for help and advice.

- Use only those prescription medicines your doctor has ordered specifically for you. Never take someone else's medicine.

- Follow your doctor's directions carefully. Take the right amount of medicine for the right number of days. Don't save prescription antibiotics.

- Read the label on any medicine carefully. Notice any warnings about side effects.

- Throw away old, or expired, medicines. Never use a medicine beyond the expiration date on the label.

One more important rule: remember to listen to and trust your body. If you think a medicine is making you sick, tell an adult. Your parents or doctor will be able to tell whether the medicine you're taking is right for you.

Medicines are meant to help you. But you must learn to use them carefully. When you do, medicines will be a part of your good health.

Glossary

analgesic   a type of medicine used to reduce or stop pain

anesthetic   a medicine that causes a loss of the sensation of pain

antibiotic   a kind of medicine that can kill bacteria that have invaded the body

antibody   a substance produced by the body's white blood cells to destroy germs that have invaded the body

antihistamine   a medicine used to relieve allergy symptoms

aspirin   a common analgesic medicine

bacteria   a group of microorganisms that can cause infectious diseases

codeine   one of several narcotic drugs

germs   a slang term for microorganisms that cause infectious diseases

histamine   a chemical produced by the body that causes allergy symptoms

immune system   the human body's natural system of self-defense

immunity   the ability to resist infection and disease

incubation   the period of time after germs have invaded the body but before they produce the symptoms of disease

lymphocyte   a type of white blood cell that identifies and marks germs that have invaded the body

medicine	a kind of drug used to fight disease and pain
microbe	another word for microorganism
microorganism	a microscopic plant or animal
morphine	one of several narcotic drugs
narcotic	a kind of drug used to reduce or stop severe pain
opiate	a group of drugs that are made from the opium poppy; also known as narcotics
over-the-counter drug	the kind of medicine that can be obtained without a doctor's prescription
pathogen	a disease-causing microorganism
phagocyte	a type of white blood cell that surrounds and destroys germs that have invaded the body
pharmacist	a person who prepares prescription medicines
prescription	a doctor's written order for a medicine
prescription medicine	the kind of medicine that can be purchased only with a doctor's written order
symptom	a warning sign or signal of disease
toxin	a poison produced by disease-causing microorganisms
vaccine	a dead or weakened dose of disease-causing bacteria or viruses that protects the body against disease
virus	a type of microorganism that causes infectious diseases

Index